Contents

Words appearing in the text in bold, **like this**, are explained in the Glossary.

 Find out more about how things are made at www.heinemannexplore.co.uk

What is in a pencil?

We use pencils for writing and drawing. This pencil has **lead** in it. The eraser on the end rubs out any mistakes.

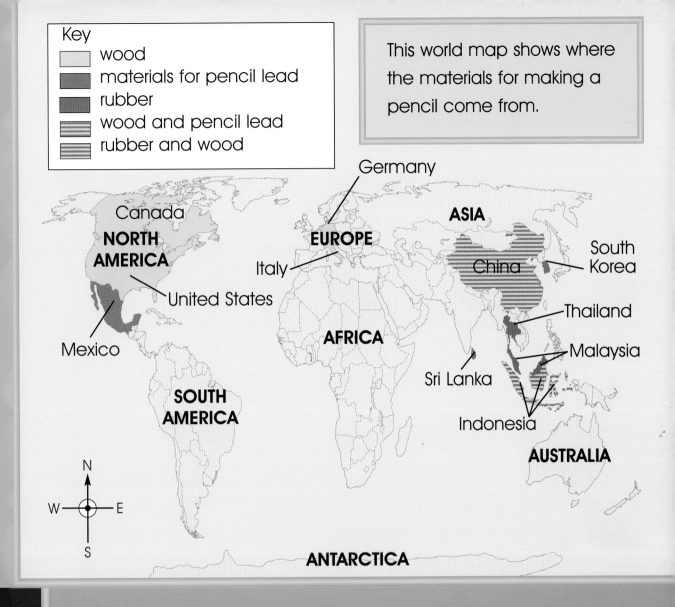

This world map shows where the materials for making a pencil come from.

Key
- wood
- materials for pencil lead
- rubber
- wood and pencil lead
- rubber and wood

A pencil is made of different **materials**. The main part is usually wood. The materials used to make pencils come from many different parts of the world.

Who makes pencils?

Several different **companies** have factories that make pencils. Many people work for each company.

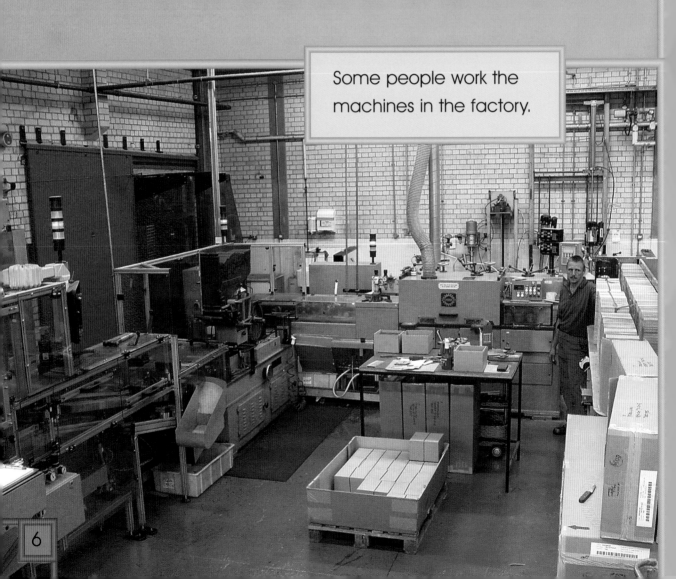

Some people work the machines in the factory.

Several people work in offices. Some of the workers decide how many pencils to make. Other workers buy the **materials** to make the pencils.

Where the wood comes from

Wood from incense cedar trees is the best wood for making pencils. The trees are cut down and left for several months. This is called seasoning.

These trees are specially grown to be made into pencils.

The wood is sawn up into thin strips called **slats**.

The thin slats of wood are soaked in **wax** and **stain**. The slats are dried and then sent to the pencil factory.

The pencil lead

The part of the pencil that marks the paper is called the **lead**, but it is not actually lead. Instead it is a mixture of **clay, graphite,** and water. The mixture is called **blacklead**.

graphite

clay

Some water is squeezed out of the mixture. The blacklead mixture is pushed through machines. The machines shape the lead into a long, thin stick. The stick is cut into strips, dried, and baked in an oven.

Hard or soft?

Some pencils have a hard **lead**. Others have a soft lead. There is more **graphite** in softer leads. Artists like to draw with the softest leads.

Stonemasons use the hardest leads to write on stone.

Most people write with HB pencils. These are hard (H) and black (B). There is more **clay** in harder leads.

13

Coloured pencils

Coloured pencils are good for drawing and colouring. The **lead** in coloured pencils is made of **clay**, **wax** and coloured **chemicals**.

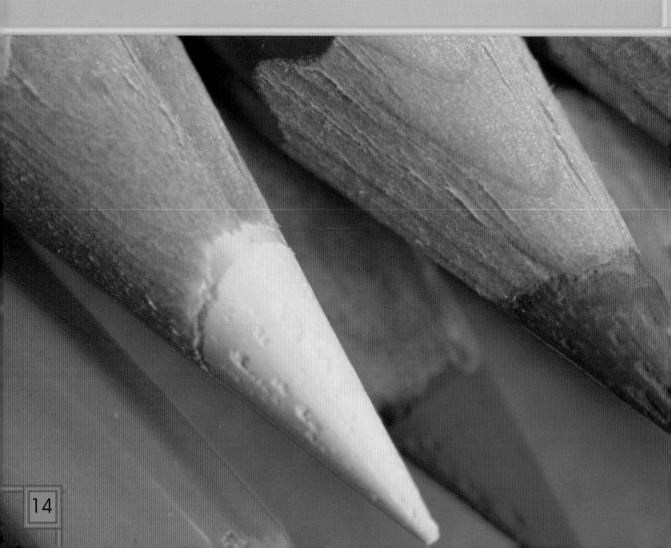

The **materials** in coloured lead are mixed together. Then they are squeezed out through a machine into a long, thin stick. The stick is not baked but left to dry in a special room.

Coloured pencils are made in many different colours.

Adding the pencil lead

Each **slat** is as long as a single pencil. Each slat is as wide as nine pencils. A machine cuts nine narrow **grooves** side by side along the slat.

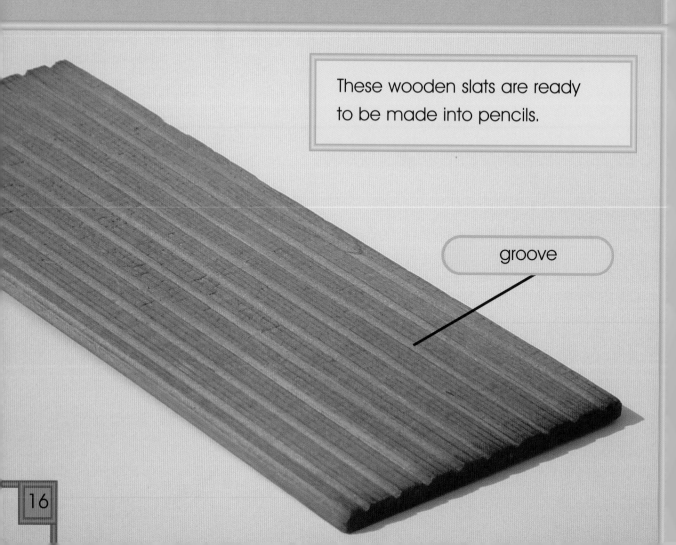

These wooden slats are ready to be made into pencils.

groove

The grooves are covered with glue.
Then a pencil **lead** is placed into each
groove. The lead is the same length as
the finished pencil.

A pencil sandwich

Grooves are cut into a second **slat**. Then this slat is placed over the first slat. The two slats are glued together to make a pencil sandwich.

Here you can see two pencil sandwiches, one above the other.

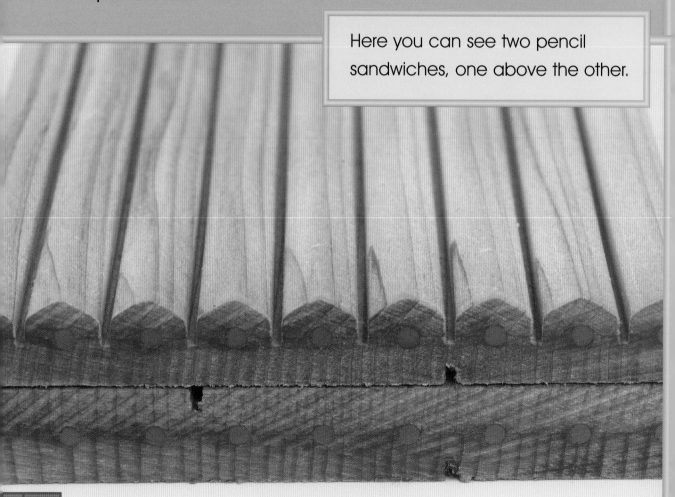

A machine cuts the pencil sandwiches into the shapes of separate pencils. Some pencils are round, but most have six flat sides.

Finishing the outside

The outside of the pencil is painted. Many pencils are painted yellow. The **company's** name is stamped on to the paint.

The letters H and B are stamped on to
show how hard and black the pencil is.
In some countries the pencil is
sharpened into a point.

The eraser

Many pencils have an eraser on the end.
The eraser is usually made of **synthetic
materials**. Some erasers are made of real
rubber.

Rubber is made from
the thick white juice
of rubber trees.

To join the eraser to the pencil, metal **bands** are put onto the end of the pencil. **Conveyor belts** carry the pencils and the metal bands to the next stage.

metal band

Joining the eraser to the pencil

A machine heats long strips of eraser. When the strips are cool, the machine cuts them into lots of small pieces.

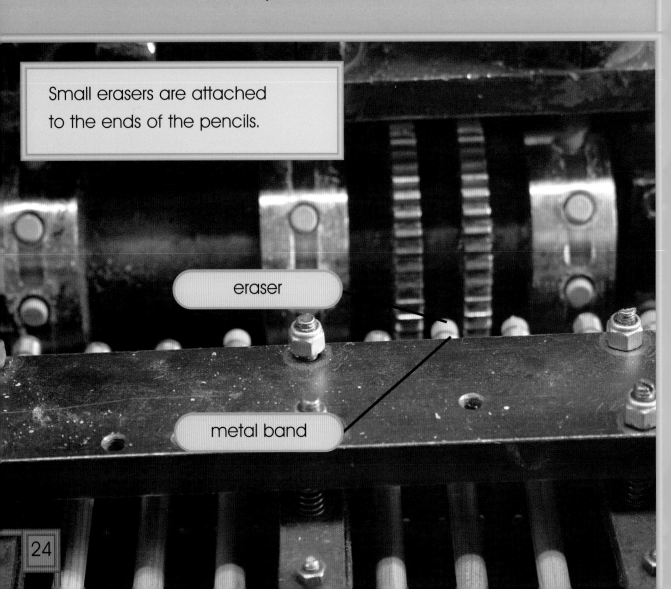

Small erasers are attached to the ends of the pencils.

eraser

metal band

The machine tightens the metal band around the eraser and the end of each pencil.

Selling the pencils

The pencils are put into boxes. A lorry takes them to a **warehouse**. They are stored in the warehouse until a shop orders some pencils.

The shop sells the pencils. Some of the money you pay goes to the pencil **company**. The pencil company uses it to make more pencils.

From start to finish

A pencil is made mainly from the wood of an incense cedar tree. The wood is cut into **slats**. **Grooves** are cut into the slats.

Leads made from **clay** and **graphite** are dropped into the grooves.

A pencil sandwich is cut into separate pencils.

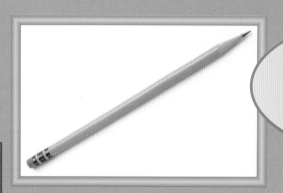

An eraser is fixed to the end of the pencil with a metal band.

A closer look

The print on the side of a pencil gives the pencil **company**'s name and the kind of lead in the pencil.

HB

type of lead

Glossary

band thin strip that is made into a loop

blacklead mixture of graphite, clay and water

chemical substance that things are made of

clay kind of mud. Clay is mainly used for making pottery.

company group of people who work together

conveyor belt machine that carries things on a long loop from one place to another

graphite soft material used to make pencil leads

groove long narrow rut

lead part of a pencil that makes a mark on paper

materials what things are made of

slat thin strip of wood

stain liquid used to colour wood and stop it from rotting

synthetic material material made from plastics or coal

warehouse building where things are stored

wax material that candles are made of

Places to visit

Catalyst, Widnes: hands-on and interactive exploration of
how the science of chemistry affects our everyday lives;
www.catalyst.org.uk

The Cumberland Pencil Museum, Keswick: journey through the
history of pencil-making:
www.pencils.co.uk

Eureka! The Museum for Children, Halifax: interactive
exhibits exploring the world of science;
www.eureka.org.uk

Glasgow Science Centre, Glasgow: fun way to learn more
about science and technology;
www.glasgowsciencecentre.org

Magna Science Adventure Centre, Rotherham: science
as an adventurous journey;
www.visitmagna.co.uk

The Science Museum, London: many special exhibitions
as well as the museum's historic collection;
www.sciencemuseum.org.uk

Scienceworks, Melbourne, Australia;
www.scienceworks.museum.vic.gov.au

Index